LEARNING BUSINESS BEGINNING EFFECTIVE STRATEGIES

JOHN LOK

Introduction

Any organizations must need management strategy. This book explains how and why organizations ought how to implement effective strategies to help them to set up their businesses more easily in the beginning. Students can understand what our businesses need real requirement in order to implement their businesses more easily and successfully in their business birth stage.

Contents

Preface

Introduction

Any organizations must need management strategy. This book explains how and why organizations ought how to implement effective strategies to help them to set up their businesses more easily in the beginning. Students can understand what our businesses need real requirement in order to implement their businesses more easily and successfully in their business birth stage.

Prologue

Table of content

Q5 Discuss the advantages and disadvantages to Google following its conversion to a plc in 2004.

Chapter 3 Cases Strategies Analysis

Q1 Explain the reason for Nike, Inc. having a mission p.20-31

Q2 Analyze two strategic objectives that Nike, Inc. might try to achieve.

Q3 Using Nike, Inc. as an example, outline the main components you might expect to see in its environment audit.

Q4 Evaluate the advantages and disadvantages to Nike, Inc. of aiming to be a socially responsibility organization.

Chapter 4 Organizational Structure Analysis

Q1 Using examples from the case study, explain the differences between internal and external stakeholders. p.32-43

Q2 Explain the benefits of any two stakeholder groups resulting from this mine project.

Q3 Explain the disadvantages to any two stakeholder groups resulting from this mine project.

Q4 Discuss the ways in which GCM could reduce the impact of the disadvantages it has created for stakeholder groups negatively affected by the mine.

Chapter 5 Organization Definition

Q1 Explain the following terms from the text:

1a Public limited company p.44-54

1b Multinational retailer

1c Technological advances

Q2 Explain how rapid economic growth in China might impact on one aspect of Carrefour's business strategy.

Q3 Analyze the social changes that may be taking place in China which could influence Carrefour's activities in China.

Q4 Produce a PEST analysis for Carrefour as it plans to open new stores in Western China.

Chapter 6 Explaining Strategies Methods

Q1 Produce a SWOT analysis for Four Season Leisure's current position. p.55-64

Q2a Construct a fully labelled decision tree showing Four Season's options.

Q2b Calculate the expected values for each option.

Q2c On financial grounds state which option Four Seasons should choose.

Q2d Analyse one weakness for Four Seasons of using decision trees as a basis for making
this business decision.

Chapter 7 Explaining Business Strategies

Q1 Use the case study to explain the difference between internal and external growth. p.65-73

Q2 Explain how the business increased sales revenue, yet gained no increase in profits for the

Q3 Assess the likely advantages and disadvantages of a cost

leadership strategy for this business.

Q4 Assess the likely advantages and disadvantages of a differentiation or a focused strategy for this business.

Chapter 8 Explaining change management strategies

Q1 define the term change management p.74-85

Q2 Explain the role a project term might have in changing the direction of HMV.

Q3 Analyze two driving forces and two restraining forces which are influencing HMV's transformation plan as it tries to change the direction of the organization.

Q4 Using an appropriate businesses model, analyse how HMV's proposed takeover of the MAMA Group will give it a competitive advantage in the music industry.

Chapter 9 Explaining international trading management strategies

Q1 Define the term globalisation p.86-93

Q2 Explain two potential advantages to Kraft of taking over Cadbury

Q3 Analyze the problems Kraft might experience as it tries to enter the European chocolate market.

Q4 Discuss how Ansoff's matrix model might have been useful to Kraft in making the decision to take over Cadbury.

CHAPTER ONE

Management/Strategic Planning Module

Q1a. Definition of entrepreneur

A business is any organization that uses resources to meet the needs of customers by providing a

product or service that they demand. Entrepreneur means an organizer who creates some

new events, organizes factors of production, undertakes risk and handles economic uncertainty

involved in new enterprise/venture. Any entrepreneur has to perform a number of functions

as a vital factor of production.

For example, Jessica wants to start a resume writing service

business who owns these personal characteristics, as hard work, desire for high

achievement, highly optimistic, independence, foresight, good organizer, innovative, time

management, effective communication, analytical ability, independence.

As Jessica is an entrepreneur who may include idea generation and scanning of the best suitable idea, determination of the business objectives, production analysis and market

research, determination of form of ownership/ organization, raising necessary funds,

recruitment, making change and business operation for whose resume writing service.

Q1b. Definition of tertiary sector business

Tertiary sector business activity firms that provide services to consumers and other businesses,

such as retailing, transport, insurance, banking, hotels, tourism and telecommunications, even

including information technological service providers.

Primary sector consists of agriculture, secondary sector is formed by industry and the

tertiary sector is incorporating all other activities that did not fit in first two sectors. For example,

Jessica's business would provide a resume writing service to individuals. Thus, the tertiary sector includes

activities such as trade and domestic activities as well as health, education ,research and development.

The four attributes that are common to service tertiary sector activities include simultaneity

between production and consumption, product intangibility, interactivity between producer and

customer/user and the idea of non-stock.

This characteristics are due to the nature of the services as a work in process, so products are

generated by the tertiary sector which may be tangible or intangible and both physical as well as

information service tertiary sector.

Q1c. Definition of finance set up

Capital consists of finance needed to set up a business any pay. For its continuing operations as

well as the man made resources used in production. These include capital goods, such as computers,

machines, factories, offices and vehicles.

Start up finance means entrepreneur gives whose cash to set up whose business capital

to operate for any business in the beginning. It is sourced either by sole trader or partner's cash or

bank loan or corporation's shares issued capital from shareholders. For example, Jessica buys office

equipments for her resume writing business or gym instructor buys gym sport equipments for

his gym sport service centre business.

Q1d. Definition of capital equipment

Business input of capital equipment is such as computers, machines, printers etc office equipments.

Some firms are capital intensive that is electricity power supply business has a high proportion of capital

equipment to other factors of production . e.g. power station. For example, the gym instructor would

need gym equipments and Jessica needs a computer in office.

Capital equipment presents tangible and fixed assets in any organizations. It means

the tangible items which are to permanently serve the business process. Capital equipment can be

consumed in one accounting period and generally are depreciated over a number of years.

Durable means of production are caused by capital equipment. During its useful life, it gives off a flow of different usages (e.g. plant equipment). The capital equipment characteristics

include organizational assets are used to supply business operations. Examples include

production line for manufacturing, testing equipment used by a construction company.

Capital equipments are typically high cost, infrequent purchases, that requires good

decision making to minimize long term costs.

Q2. Outline of production factors of production needed to set up the business providing to school leavers.

For this resume writing service to school leavers business of Jessica, its factors of production

may include that the entrepreneur (capital) uses to pay office rent, electricity, water, buying office equipments,

printers and computers and stationary etc general office operational expenditure ; (land) she rents

an office or may work at home to let every school leaver to know where who can give individual working

experiences and educational background information to Jessica to help them to write individual resume;

(labour) Jessica can choose either to work for herself or she can employ employees to assist her.

employing writing resume skilful writers will be intangible asset if who can help her to attract many school

leavers. Instead of employing writing resume assistant, Jessica could also employ cleaner, office receipt,

accounting clerk staffs if she needed.

Finally, the factor of production includes Jessica is a (enterpriser) herself who needs to manage and control

and give ideas how to operate her writing resume service business efficiently and effectively every day.

Q3. Business functions of gum instructor's business

I recommend that gym instructor's gym sport service centre business ought include these departments:

(a) Marketing department can research different gym sport service competitors' prices to measure

what service fee charging is the most reasonable service fee. It aims to compare their gym sport service quality,

the satisfactory level of clients' feeling to play sport bicycles and running machines etc equipment and

gym instructor serving attitude to get the most reasonable service fee. Marketing department can design

the suitable different payment plans to provide clients to choose payment methods.

After clients use gym sport bicycles and running machines etc equipments from gym instructors

instruction, who can choose either to pay service fee per hour or choose to join to be monthly or

annual member to pay discount service fee. Thus, I recommend who need to employ at least one

market research staff to research the competitors' different service quality and every client

satisfaction level to evaluate what is its reasonable price every month.

(b) Finance department can record and analyse his gym business accounting

financial information. For example: Purchasing sport bicycles and running machines etc sport

centre equipments expenditure, staff salary, rent, electricity, water, insurance etc expenditure.

(c) Human resource department can identify the work force needs, recruits, selects and trains appropriate staff.

For example, employing at least one gym service manager gym instructor or gym instructing trainee, cashier, cleaner positions when his business expands.

(d) Customer service department can help every individual to register member record, cashing, answering enquiry etc front line service in gym sport service centre.

(e) Operating management department can manage gym sport service operation to ensure to satisfy individual need successfully.

Q4. Explain reasons why most enterprisers choose to set up the tertiary sector business

Enterprisers prefer to choose to set up tertiary sector business. The reasons are as below:

Firstly, Developed countries is declining in the importance of secondary sector activity and an increase in the

tertiary sector. It is known as deindustrialisation. Rising incomes associated with higher living standards

have led consumers to spend much of their extra income on services rather than more goods.

These developed countries' people need more entertainment to become their social habits.

Thus, hotel, travel, restaurant, cinema, music, internet etc entertainment tertiary sector businesses

will increase demand in these developed countries.

Secondly, Manufacturing workers may find it different to find employment in other sector of industry and it causes structural unemployment. Manufacturing businesses in the developed countries face much more competition and these competitors tend to be more efficient and use cheaper labour. Moreover, technological innovation causes new technological products import demand increasingly. For example, laptop computers, desk computers, mobiles etc high technological products will increase demand because developed countries' people have afford money to buy these products commonly. It rises import and domestic secondary sector firms have been forced to close.

Thirdly, enterprisers don't require large amounts of capital to buy capital equipments if who choose to do tertiary sector service or trading businesses.

Finally, some enterprisers rely on their past tertiary sector business experience own skills and interest. Thus, It implies entrepreneurs have more opportunities to choose to set up service or trading tertiary sector businesses in any developed countries market nowadays.

CHAPTER TWO

Partnership definition

Q1 Explains the term of partnership

A partnership is a collaborative relationship between two or more people to work toward shared objectives

through a mutually agreed division of labour. Partners can deliver of practical solutions at the strategic level

to carry on business together, with shared capital investment and usually shared responsibilities.

The characteristics of partnership include a shared leadership among individuals who are empowered

by own organizations and trusted by partners to resolve conflicts, a shared common vision and purpose

that recognizes value contribution of all members and acceptance of differences (e.g. values, ways of

working) is key components of a successful partnership.

Q2 Outline two benefits to Larry Page and Sergey Brin of starting Google as a partnership.

The two benefits to Larry Page and Sergey Brin of starting Google as a partnership include these

two hands.

They can exchange their individuals with networking skills, sharing information, coordinating efforts, transferred or combined service and governance and resources to concentrate on managing themselves

internet commerce field to operate partnership together. Hence, they can achieve strategic alliance benefit of

decision making power is shared or transferred. Management of a program or mutual interest to participating

organizations' missions to reduce risk by one internet technological firm itself.

The another hand, their business losses can shared and additional capital can injected by each partner to have

enough capital to expand their internet technological business in the short term.

Q3 Examine the difficulties the partners would have encountered when they set up Google.

The difficulties the partners would have encountered when they set up Google which can include these two

factors of external competitive environment and internal organization cooperation factors.

On the internal organization cooperation factor, they can exist different vision and ideas to operate whether

one partner dominates or partners compete for the lead, lack of understanding role and responsibilities and lack

of support from partner organizations with decision making power and difference of philosophies and manners

of working and lack of commitment and unwilling participants and financial and time commitment outweigh

potential benefits and too little time for effective consultation and spending much time to get trust to build long

term partnership relationship and employees need time to adapt new organizational culture and change

management between of them during they set up Google in the beginning together.

For example problems include that design company logo and administration and managing employee

cooperation and deciding what users are looking for from their websites and how to calculate page's room

housed in their servers and how to make users spend as little time as possible on their website search etc

problems. When they set up Google internet technological business in the beginning.

On the external competitive environment factor, it faced the Yahoo internet technological monopoly.

It provided email service, news headlines, a website directory, advertisement, webpage hosting and

other online services to different countries. Yahoo sources of revenue include sale of

advertisement space, paid premium, content and extended service commission for sale made through

its online stores and park link placement. Hence, these two partners set up partnership which need have

unique internet service to win their this Yahoo competitor in this internet commerce market in the beginning.

Q4 Explain the term public limited company (plc).

Public limited company is incorporated legal form of organization to run business. Companies are

incorporated to form an entity with a separate legal personality. This means that the organization can do business and enter into contracts in its own name.

A public limited company is owned by its members (shareholders), who have invested in the business and

enjoy limited liability. For example, the company's finances are separate from the personal finances of owners.

It has legal right to sell shares to the general public. Its shard price is quoted on the national stock exchange.

Q5 Discuss the advantages and disadvantages to Google following its conversion to a plc in 2004.

Although, Google changed to public limited company form from partnership in 2004 and it's revenue

sources must not be changed after 2004. Generally, Google drives its revenue for two sources: Sale of its

research technology to other companies and sale of advertisement space on its search result pages.

However, it will still have advantages and disadvantages to a public limited company in 2004.

It's advantages include it was a partnership and it can't issue shares to public to increase capital before. After

2004, it formed a public limited company, it can ease of buying and selling of shares for shareholders to

encourage investment and access to substantial capital sources due to the ability to issue a prospectus to the

public and to offer shares for sale, public limited company can have separate legal entity and limited liability to

Google.

Otherwise, public limited company also have these disadvantages include it needs legal formalities in formation, cost of business consultants and financial advisers when creating it, share prices subject to

fluctuation, sometimes for seasons beyond business's control from poor economy, legal requirements

concerning disclosure of information to shareholders and the public, e.g. annual publication of detailed report

and accounts, risk of takeover due to the availability of the shares on the stock exchange and directors

are influenced by short-term objectives of major investors.

CHAPTER THREE

Cases Strategies Analysis

Q1 Explain the reason for Nike, Inc. having a mission

A mission statement is a statement of the organization's purpose, what it wants to accomplish in the larger environment.

The reasons for Nike , Inc needs a mission statement as below:

(a) Nike, Inc. is a sport products trading company. it needs have a clear mission statement because

Nike, Inc. can know what it's business is, who it's clients are, what clients value do and what it's

business should be these questions to achieve its business intention more successful if it had a clear mission

statement . Thus, its stakeholders can know core purpose and activity in a short paragraph.

For example, it's mission statement is to bring inspiration and innovation to every athlete in the world of

whose every body and who can become athlete successfully.

(b) The reason for it needs have a mission statement include it can give message to let Nike's clients and employees to know what it's products can attribute in global sport product market, it should be translated into supporting objectives for each level management and create a hierarchy of objectives that are consistent with one another within organization, Nike's objectives are followed the mission statement. All mission statement can influence it's objective can be achieved. Thus, it can recognise the markets and benefits of serving these sport markets.

(c) It can give ethical reference to motivate employees by identifying positive core goals.

Q2 Analyze two strategic objectives that Nike, Inc. might try to achieve.

Nike, Inc was formed as an importer of Japanese shoes, 1962. Today, Nike was holding a global market share of approximately 37% (Puma.com) In the United States, it's sport products were sold through about 22,000 retail accounts; world wide, it's products were sold in more than 160 countries. It developed to sell of athletic footwear, apparel and equipment, which together approximately $18,6 million in sales during Nike's 2008 year. It divided its products into four segments: footwear, apparel, sport equipment and other products. In 2008, these segments accounted for 52%, 28%, 6% and 14% of Nike's revenue respectively (Adidas Group.com). In addition to manufacturing sportswear and equipment, it operated retails stores the Nike town name. Nike's competitors, like New Balance, but also against large athletic footwear and manufacture like Adidas AG and Puma. Thus it implied Nike had good strategic planning to achieve it's sale objective before.

However, I think Nike should have these problems which would encounter in the future. For example,

although Nike always represents high quality and highly reliable. However, the cost will be higher than other

brands. The public feels that Nike overcharges its consumers and should reduce the price of their products

and it had any new sport products to develop because clients‘ taste are varied from time to time and it's

sport products' life cycle are getting short and clients can have a wide range of selection from running

shoes or sunglasses with Nike brand in the future and fake products could be one of the most critical

reasons for Nike. In fact, in some Asia countries: Taiwan, China or Vietnam. Nike could lose more than

million dollars because they don't have effective way to stop those take products.

There should be specific , measurable, achievable, realistic and time specific and should be based on the

corporate aims.

However, I shall recommend these two strategic objective that Nike, Inc. might try to achieve.

Strategic planning means the process of developing and maintaining a strategic fit between the

organization's goals and capabilities and its changing marketing opportunities.

The first strategic objective , it can raise sales by 5% by end of the year. It's methods can include that

Nike might try to analyze it's current business portfolio of sport running shoes and sport equipments etc products to judge different countries' clients' number of age group segments to buy their different product

numbers in the future. This strategic objectives is to create value for Nike Inc. clients and build clients

relationship by market segmentation and targeting.

Hence, on the strategic level, Nike Inc. might design business portfolio in its strategy. Business portfolio

is the collection of businesses and products that make up it. Thus, Nike Inc. must analyze its

current business portfolio or strategic business units and decide which strategic business units

should receive more or less or should downsize its business portfolio by eliminating some style of

sport running shoes and equipment etc products designs of business units that are not profitable

or that no longer fit Nike's overall strategy.

Another method include that differentiation is creating superior customer value by actually differentiating the

market offering and positioning is arranging for a product to occupy a clear, distinctive and desirable place

relative to competing products in the minds of target consumers.

Nike might try to diversify to produce more new style and design sport running shoes and new sport

equipments product numbers to attract more clients to choose to buy its sport products. This market strategy is

differentiation and positioning in global sport product markets, aim to win its competitors. For example: Old

styles in new colour athletic running shoes.

The another strategic objective, Nike can achieve all new sport products developed during the year

should use materials from natural sources and it can carry out an environmental audit of the sport product range by the end of the year.

Its methods can include that Nike can cut greenhouse gas emissions by 10% in all factories by the end

of year and all new sport products developed during the year should use materials from natural sources or

renewable resources and use suppliers who are socially responsible and implementation of the common

high standards for the wellbeing of all employees. For example, giving fair salary to factories workers,

willingness to pay cost of environment protection and establishment and implementation of ethical codes

of practice to become a socially responsible organization.

Reference

Financial reports (2009), PUMA.com, http://about.puma.com/EN/5/35/35/.

Income statement (2009), Adidas Group, http;//adidas-group.corporate-publications.com/en/group-management-report/income-statement-7.html.

Q3 Using Nike, Inc. as an example, outline the main components you might expect to see in its environment audit.

Nike, Inc.'s factories need have safety and clean working environment for their workers to work

and reduce air and water pollution to natural environment from its plastic wastage to

damage natural environment to influence different countries stakeholders of citizen health.

Its plastic wastage pollution level is very serious to influence the manufacturing countries

stakeholders of citizen health daily. Hence, its environment audit needs outline these main components as below:

. Use of renewable resources to make the sport products.

. Implementation of common high standards for the wellbeing of all employees.

. use suppliers who are socially responsible.

. Implementation of long term socially responsible aim rather than short term profit objectives.

. Willingness to pay cost of environmental protection.

. Establishment and implementation of ethical codes of practice to become a socially responsible organization.

Q4 Evaluate the advantages and disadvantages to Nike, Inc. of aiming to be a socially responsibility organization.

Nike, Inc needs to be a socially responsibility organization to concern its stakeholders of consumers,

employees, environment benefit. Nike, Inc was a organization to become more increasing global,

it is becoming more difficult to ensure ethical to supply chain and takes on ethical approach to

managing the workplace that extends beyond organizational national and cultural boundaries.

For example, Nike, Inc. has strong research and development apartments is because Nike's sport products are

manufactured in low wage factories in the far East countries. Therefore they can concentrate on

marketing image and research project. However, it's low salary workers need have human right

protection to rise their reasonable wage level. Thus it is not a socially responsibility organization, it

needs to implement a socially responsibility organization to make stakeholders to believe in the future.

However, it will have advantages and disadvantages during it plan to achieve a social responsibility organization.

On advantages hand, it can promote good public image, it is pride of employees can be a motivator,

it is being ahead of changes in law which can give time to find cheaper solution and it can avoid

costly bad media publicity on damaging natural environment issues.

On the disadvantages hand, it needs to increase cost to produce new sport products, it needs to take

manpower and attention from other important aims and objectives, it's result will be long teem rather than

short term, stakeholders will be conflict on socially responsible and ethical issues and it is possible that

it will drop in profit due to increase costs and may have negative effect on share prices.

CHAPTER FOUR

Organizational Structure Analysis

Q1 Using examples from the case study, explain the differences between internal and external stakeholders.

Stakeholders are groups of people or individual who can be affected or is affected to gain advantages or

disadvantages by the achievement of purpose and action taken by an organization. Stakeholders can be

individuals, communities, social groups organizations. For example, stakeholders in a forest policy might

include people who live in or near the relevant forests, people who live further away who live further

away who use those forests, settlers from where in the country or abroad.

British GCM Co does mining/coal project scheme in Bangladesh country.

It's internal stakeholders are people who own or work for it's mining/coal project in Bangladesh country. For

example, shareholders, managers, workers, directors etc all staffs.

It's external stakeholders are people who do not work for

or own a business for it's mining/coal project scheme in Bangladesh country. For example, Bangladesh country Government, the world development movement organization, the Asian development bank loan lender, local residents, international campaign groups, local newspapers and TV channels, local farmers and landowners etc.

Q2 Explain the benefits of any two stakeholder groups resulting from this mine project.

Stakeholders group have benefits from GCM Co mine project scheme in Bangladesh country which include GCM employees, GCM shareholders, landowners, Asian development bank, suppliers etc.

GCM Co needs invest large expansion of its coal/mining business project by building a new head office and coal/mine site to develop natural resource in Bangladesh country.

Possible benefits impact on Bangladesh country central and/or local Government which larger new head office will lead to increase payments to Bangladesh country local Government through local business taxation , a mining project would provide a boost to the Bangladesh country economy, a lot of tonnes of coal would be exported, it brings a valuable foreign currency for the economy. The mine/coal could also supply cheap coal for power generation in Bangladesh country providing a cheap source of electricity and further boosting the economy. Jobs would also be created, helping the Government to achieve its macro economies objectives as well as local community, the mine project would employment and a some of income to members of the local population. This income will be spent on local services and goods, further benefiting the local community.

Possible benefits impact on Bangladesh country suppliers of information technology to provide service to GCM Co to help them to earn more income because it needs new information technology coal/mine productive machines to rise coal workers efficiency and shorten time to produce coal production. It may lead to reduce mining/coal nature waste to produce more coal/mining natural resource from information technological machines. Thus, it can raise to sell more coal/mining numbers from high information technological machines to earn more profit to shareholders.

Q3 Explain the disadvantages to any two stakeholder groups resulting from this mine project.

The mine/coal project needs much lands physically and economically displace many people. This displacement will take place in one of the most densely populated countries in the world and will destroy a critical agricultural region in the Bangladesh country.

It will cause disadvantages to local community, the environmental damage is caused by mining, it would be indicated by land development movement. The mining would spoil landscape and cause diversion of a river and destruction of a forest, will resulting impact on those who depend on the forest for making living. For example, farmers and local community homes would have to be relocated.

It will cause disadvantages to it's employees, the mining/ coal project may being employees into conflict

with the local community and who are against the mine/coal job. Although workers need the work, who

may feel uncomfortable about the significant destruction of environment being caused by the mining/ coal

project.

Q4 Discuss the ways in which GCM could reduce the impact of the disadvantages it has created for stakeholder groups negatively affected by the mine.

GCM co can reduce impact of disadvantages , it has created for stakeholder groups negatively affected

by mining/coal project scheme in Bangladesh country.

They include that workers whose homes are moved, so GCM Co can offer compensation and it can build better

home for them, landowners who have land forcibly purchased, so GCM Co can offer more than the current

market price and arrange meetings to explain that they will be compensated, farmers whose land now has no

water due to relocated river, so GCM Co can offer compensation and/or jobs in the new mining/coal to

family members.

CHAPTER FIVE

Organization Definition

Q1 Explain the following terms from the text:

1a Public limited company

Public limited company means an incorporated limited liability business whose shares are traded

publicly on the stock exchange and whose reports and accounts are publicly available.

1b Multinational retailer

This is a chain of shops that operates in various countries in addition to the country in which its

headquarters is located.

1c Technological advances

These are innovations in machinery, equipment or computer systems which may allow the

business to improve efficiency of operation and /or economies of scale.

Q2 Explain how rapid economic growth in China might impact on one aspect of Carrefour's business

strategy.

Business planning is a management-directed process of identifying long-term goals for a business or

business segment, and formulating realistic strategies for reaching those goals. Through planning,

HYPERLINK "http://www.referenceforbusiness.com/encyclopedia/Kor-Man/Management.html" management decides what objectives to pursue during a future period, and what actions to undertake

to achieve those objectives.

Carrefour was the world's first department store opened in Paris, France in 1959. Although it didn't

enter China market unteil 1995, the speed of its development in China has been faster than any other

countried. To June of 2006, Carrefour had established 78 chain stores in China, starting with

first store in Beijing, Carrefour arrived in Shanghai and Shenzhen in 1996.

Carrefour developed so rapidly in China because China can offer it very good economic benefit

and development of Carrefour in China has realized economies of scale. Thus, Carrefour one aspect of

business strategy is to such as the establishment of distribution centres to reduce transport and

distribution costs to expand more supermarket in China different cities.

For example, Carrefour's supermarkets have established special counters for quality line foods.

They havea clear brand logo, foods are packaged, not only quality line label, but also with supplier

information on a traceable barcode. The quality line is control and supervision by Carrefour raw

and freash agribulture food throughout the supply chain from planting and processing to distribution, in order to guarantee the quality and safety of foods of Carrefour own brand.

The quality line has a number a key aims to maintain traceability throughout the supply chain from planting to eating, to produce agriculture food with no pesticide reside, to ensure quality is consistent and reliable, to use environment friendly production and processing technologoes and produce at a price acceptable to market to be lower than truly organic food because only a few consumers can afford organiz food.

It decentralized management. It divided its Chinese to structure into four regions of East China, South China, North China and middle China. It used local partners, such as Shanghainese partner

in Shanghai, a Cantonese partner in Guangzhou and a Beijing partner in Beijing. It also employed China storemanagers to manage it's supermarkets, their duties include foods on orders, purchasing, pricing supplier selection, arrangement and store displays, employees recruitment and negotiating promotional campaigns etc. Employing foreign Chineses to manage its supermarkets in China is more acceptable to it local clients in China.

Moreover, Carrefour has a variety of cooperative ways of working with agriculture food suppliers in China by joint operation. Thus, Carrefour business strategy competes against its supermarket competitors on the basic of price, convenience and customer experience.

In conclusion, this business strategy is such as the establishment of distribution centres in China, it

achieved Carrefour could expanded established 78 chain stores in China in 2006.

Q3 Analyze the social changes that may be taking place in China which could influence Carrefour's

activities in China.

Since the mid-1990 year, changes have taken place in consumers' demands for agriculture food in

China, citizen's incomes have increased rapidly, rapid growth of Gross domestic product per capita.

People's food demands have changed from quantity to quality, safety and diversity, rise in education levels

and improvement in social welfare and improved communication with other countries.

The first supermarkets were developed rapidly in China from 1990 and China's entry into the world

trading to begin to open its retail market in general and in 2004 foreign businesses entered China's market and

the increasing competition among and between supermarkets and traditional retail stores.

China consumers traditionally buy raw and fresh agriculture food every day. So the quality and availability

of raw and fresh agriculture food has become an important measurement of supermarkets' attractiveness

to clients. Many supermarkets provide organic and green agriculture foods in their stores too (Hu, D. 2005).

Because China economic growth to cause social changes, it could influence Carrefour carried on these activities sell its agriculture foods in its China supermarkets as below:

Although economic development and improvement in people's living standards, China customers demand the quality of raw and fresh agriculture food and choice of varieties and safety agriculture food in China are rising. Thus, Carrefour classifies these raw and fresh agriculture food into five categories: Fish, meat, fruit and vegetables, salads and breads. Carrefour must keep these foods to save in clean and cold store room to keep all foods to be fresh to prepare to sell to it's clients from Fresh transportation process.

China social changes cause it has many diverse cultures and consumers. For example, Beijing drink beer social changes adapt to local tastes and preferences in these areas. Carrefour introduces new products, such as wine to China and promotes wine fairs and educates Chinese how to drink wine and what foods it goes with. Carrefour imports wine to Chinese to adapt to local taste or by using its knowledge from Taiwan.

Carrefour's selling strategies also be changed to adapt to sell fish alive and sell frozen fish to the China bigger cities preferred to buy fish alive, right out of fish tanks. Chinese west and middle China preferred to purchase frozen fish because they are further away from the coast and want fish to be fresh. Thus China social changes also change Carrefour's fish sale behaviour in China supermarkets to adapt to local consumer and shopping behaviours.

Rising Asian middle class and China consumers are more conscience of health and environment and Carrefour
can have its own line of organic foods and it stocks fair trade products and it has also reduced energy
energy consumption and disposable plastic bag numbers in China is a opportunity to Carrefour to do food sale
business.

In conclusion, China social changes brought Chinese consumers like to compare different brands. Thus,
Carrefour must introduce larger shelves in order to place all different brands in one areas in supermarkets.

Reference

Hu, Dinghuan (2005), On the binary structure of agriculture food: The impact of supermarket development
on the agriculture sector and agriculture food safety, Chinese Rural Economy, no.2 pp.12-17.

Q4 Produce a PEST analysis for Carrefour as it plans to open new stores in Western China.

PEST analysis elements include political, economic, social and technological aspects.

As Carrefour plans to open new stores in Western China. It needs to produce a PEST analysis to help it
to know China external environments factors to affect it's business objective and strategies to achieve
its business aim in China supermarket market successfully.

On the political aspect, China opens world trading market

to let different countries investors to establish their businesses in Western China. This Carrefour can enter China supermarket market more easily.

On the economic aspect, the current devaluation of the Euro will import more expensive to European businesses. This is a threat to Carrefour to enter western market, Rising Asian middle class in Western China can increase supermarket food purchase demand.

On the social aspect, Western China consumers are more conscience of health and environment and Carrefour can have its own line of organic foods and it stocks fair trade products and it has also reduced energy energy consumption and disposable plastic bag numbers in Western China. It is a opportunity to Carrefour to do supermarket business in Western China.

On the technological aspect, social networking sites provide an opportunity for Carrefour supermarket because which can be used to increase customer loyalty to brand, e.g. twitter and face book can be used to create commonly for loyal of Carrefour's clients in Western China easily.

CHAPTER SIX

Explaining Strategies Methods

Q1 Produce a SWOT analysis for Four Season Leisure's current position.

A SWOT analysis is a form of strategic analysis that identifies and analyses the internal strengths and weaknesses and external opportunities and threats that will influence the future direction and success of a business. Thus, a SWOT analysis provides information that can be helpful in matching the firm's resources and strengths to the competitive environment in which it operates. It is useful in strategy formation and selection.

Four Season Leisure's SWOT analysis for current position as below:

Internal strengths: Thirty years of providing holidays to high income European and North American consumers travel business experiences to build most famous brands in the Caribbean, it has attributed the group's relative success to effective management from a team of people that have considerable knowledge and expertise in the travel market.

Internal Weaknesses: It's concentration in the Caribbean travel market is weakness.

External opportunities: The world economic slow down and It causes traveller demands decrease,

expanding into some of the new destinations that its customers are interested in visiting.

External threats: Increasing Four Season Leisure's share of the travel market, all inclusive holiday resort

market, The competition is from new holiday destination such as Dubai.

Q2a Construct a fully labelled decision tree showing Four Season's options.

Four Season's decision tree economic conditionsinitial cost projected profit
expected value
Option 1: Open new resort ($120 million) fast growth $40 million x20%
in Dubai

normal growth $200 million x 50%

recession -($100 million x 30%)

Option 2: Open new resort
in Thailand ($150 million) fast growth $500 million x 20%

normal growth $300 million x 50%

recession -($50 million x 30%)

Option 3: Upgrade existing ($80 million) fast growth $150 million x 20%
existing resorts
in Caribbean normal growth $120 million x 50%

recession -(%100 million x 30%)

Q2b Calculate the expected values for each option.

Four Season leisure expected values as below:

Option 1

fast growth $40 million x20% + normal growth $200 million x 50% - recession ($100 million x 30%)

Thus option 1 expected value is $78 million

Option 2

fast growth $500 million x 20% + normal growth $300 million x 50% - recession ($50 million x 30%)

Thus option 2 expected value is $235 million

Option 3

fast growth $150 million x 20% + normal growth $120 million x 50% - recession ($100 million x 30%)

Thus option 3 expected value is $ 60 million

Q2c On financial grounds state which option Four Seasons should choose.

Four Season Leisure will choose option 2 because it's expected value is $ 235 million and it's

economic condition initial cost is $150 million, it can earn predict profit is $85 million.

However, the other two options is both initial cost amount is much than expected value

, so it have predicted loss.

Q2d Analyse one weakness for Four Seasons of using decision trees as a basis for making
this business decision.

Decision trees is a technique that considers the value of the options available and the chance of them occurring. It is a diagram that sets out the options connected with a decision and the

outcomes and economic returns that may result.

Four Season leisure uses decision trees to make business decision to predict which travel

destination option can earn the largest expect value, if it evaluates the fast growth,

normal growth and recession occurrence chance is wrong, it will choose the expect value

is not the nest financial return. Thus decision trees has possible the incorrect fast growth,

normal growth and recession to predict for these travel destination expect value.

CHAPTER SEVEN

Explaining organizational strategies

Q1 Use the case study to explain the difference between internal and external growth.

Traffic clothing plc produces suits and dresses and sells them to major retailers in several

countries. It plan to grow it's clothing manufacturing business to overseas.

Internal growth can be achieved in a number of ways and these forms of growth can lead

to differing effects on stakeholder groups, such as customers, workers and competitors.

Reasons include to plan these internal growth strategy of sale turnover have grown

by around 15% each year, but a slower rate than some competitors, aims to increase

much profit. For example, Traffic clothing plc plans to open own clothing retailer shops in towns and cities to offer customers a top quality shopping experience to allow

suits and dresses differentiation in a crowded markets , aims to increase market

share in clothing industry. Increased economic of scale of internal growth strategy,

traffic low prices have been possible due to the opening of low cost factories in

developing countries.

External growth means business expansion is achieved by means of merging with or

taking over another business from either the same or a different industry.

It's external growth strategy could be achieved by aggressive takeover either other

clothing producers or material suppliers to achieve cost leadership, it would focused on a

small, higher in come market segment in several overseas markets.

This could be reinforced with a merger with a prestige clothing retailer.

Q2 Explain how the business increased sales revenue, yet gained no increase in profits for the last three years.

Traffic clothing plc can increased sale revenue by around 15% each year, yet gained to increase in

profits for the last three years.

The reasons include these factors, new competitors were entering the clothing market and driving down

prices, raw material prices for both natural and man-made inputs were rising, the number of merger between

large clothing retailers had increased that bargaining power when dealing with producers like Traffic.

Q3 Assess the likely advantages and disadvantages of a cost leadership strategy for this business.

The advantages and disadvantages of a cost leadership strategy for Traffic clothing plc manufacturing

business as below:

Cost leadership strategy means the lowest cost producer in the industry for a certain level of product

quality will allow the firm to make higher profits than competitors or if the businessman lowers its

prices below the average of competitors, to increase market share. This strategy usually targets a broad

rather than a niche market, e.g. Ryanair, one of Europe's largest and most profitable airlines, is also

the lowest average cost airline. Thus, traffic clothing plc adapts this cost leadership strategy either producers

suits and dresses due to opening of low cost factories in developing countries to sell to major retailers in

several countries at average industry prices to earn higher profit than clothing competitors or below

industry average prices to gain market share.

The cost leadership advantages to Traffic clothing plc include that it can spend more extra money to invest

to buy of high level of advanced clothing production machines to shorten time of the clothing manufacturing

process in efficient production methods for rise to produce many suits and dresses numbers to sell to major

retailers in several countries, economic of scale to produce suits and dresses to reduce clothing manufacturing

cost for long time.

However, cost leadership strategy also has these disadvantages to Traffic clothing plc includes that it could be

achieved b aggressive takeover of either other clothing producers or material suppliers to achieve cost

leadership if it expanded its clothing manufacturing business by means of merging to them to taking one

another business from either the clothing manufacturing industry or clothing retail industry.

Thus, it would give cost leadership benefits to it's competitors in clothing manufacturers or

clothing retailers.

Q4 Assess the likely advantages and disadvantages of a differentiation or a focused strategy for this business.

The advantages and disadvantages of a differentiation or a focused strategy for Traffic clothing plc as below:

Differentiation strategy advantages involves developing a product or service that offers unique features valued

clients.

Traffic clothing plc can own clothing retail shops in itself and several countries to offer customers a

top quality shopping experience, this will allow differentiation in a crowed market.

Traffic clothing plc can rise suits and dresses sale value added to its clothing product or provide training

to raise sale people service performance by these features may allow it to charge a premium price for it

when it's clients feel a top quality shopping experience from its sale people service performance. It can

help strong sales team able to promote the perceived strengths of its brand and its suits and dresses clothing

products, rising Traffic clothing plc corporate reputation for innovation and quality and it can have extra money to prepare excellent research and development clothing manufacturing machine facilities.

However, differentiation strategy has disadvantages to it, it needs spend much money to invest
to buy high speed and advanced clothing manufacturing technological machines to help it to rise to
produce high quality and unique of suits and dresses clothing products in the short time and it needs
to lend loan from banks if it has no enough capital to buy these clothing manufacturing machines.

The focused strategy concentrates on a narrow market segment, aiming to achieve either a cost
advantages or differentiation. This can lead to a high degree of customer loyalty within the market
segment.

Traffic clothing plc focused strategy could be achieved by aggressive takeovers of either other
clothing producers or material suppliers to achieve cost leadership, focusing on a smaller, higher
income market segment. This could be reinforced with a merger with a prestige clothing
retailer.

Advantages include Traffic clothing plc can concentrate on sell its suits and dresses clothing
products to several countries, eg. young age between 20 to 40 male or female group clients.

However, disadvantages include, it needs to time to gather information about it's client age target to choose
which major several countries and the young age group in different countries of clients .

If it's clothing sale numbers reduced, even it will have too many old clothing stocks to keep in its warehouse,

it has no power to sell these old clothing stocks for long time.

These old clothing stocks would be obsolete, it's clients won't willing to accept to buy old style clothing or

damaged clothing in warehouse to keep long time.

CHAPTER EIGHT

Explaining change management strategies

Q1 define the term change management

Change management involves planning, implementing, controlling, and reviewing the movement of an organization from its current state to a new one.

The change management includes external and internal factors. Planned change results from deliberate decisions to alter an organization and unplanned change is imposed on the organization and is often unforeseen.

Internal forces for change include things like declining effectiveness (resignations or major accidents), changes in employee expectations and changes in the work climate, e.g. organizations need to develop and improve reasons.

External forces for change include globalization, workforce diversity, technological innovation, ethics. Change may take one of three forms, incremental change is relatively small in scope and as such, results in small improvements. Strategic change is a larger scale approach that is similar to a restructuring effort.

Thus, change management moves the organization forward a different and sometimes, unknown future state.

Q2 Explain the role a project term might have in changing the direction of HMV.

Change management is a complex and large subject area which tends to form part of higher level questions.

Project team means a group of employees entrusted with managing a defined project (this may be a change

management project). The team may consist of special employees required from the success of the

new project.

Thus HMV music entertainment business project team role and responsibilities may include:

Identification of areas of change, e.g. changing by acquisition, pure MHV loyalty card scheme, 50%

stake in 7 digital, pilot HMV (Urzon -branded cinema in Wimbledon), establishment of new vision

and objectivity to design new organization management structure to adapt new management structure

after HMV music entertainment business takeovers HAMA Group, ensuring resources are enough to used

in planning change, e.g. timing, legal, marketing development etc requiring, implementing and controlling

and reviewing if planning process and reducing conflict avoidance measures and education of major

shareholders. e.g. HMV music entertainment business major shareholders who must need to approve the

MAMA music entertainment Group major shareholders offer during their communication must be needed to

involve in their every time board of meeting in decision making process, project team needs to support staffs,

giving negotiation, reducing threatening where there is still restrain to them.

Q3 Analyze two driving forces and two restraining forces which are influencing HMV's transformation plan as it tries to change the direction of the organization.

Driving forces which are influencing it (HMV company) tries to change the direction of organization successfully include: falling sales and growth of illegal download is existing in music entertainment market, which may make internal stakeholders more willing to co-operate, as well as management enthusiasm is for expanding into live music as a new marker. These is external and internal factors support to achieve takeover planning is successfully.

Restraining forces which are influencing it (HMV company) tries to takeover MAMA Group to change direction of organization successfully. HMV company may not be recognized as player in the live music market because it lacks management expertise in the cinema market and artist areas and MAMA Group which is focus on these market areas, instead of music area; HMV's takeover offer for MAMA Group is subject to approval from shareholders, who are concerned about HMV moving into a market where it has limited direct experience, along with prospects of raising finance to fund the takeover. This contrasts with the enthusiastic view of HMV's management who are keen to explore the prospects of live music as a new market. These are external and internal factors threat to implement takeover planning successfully.

Q4 Using an appropriate businesses model, analyse how HMV's proposed takeover of the

MAMA Group will give it a competitive advantage in the music industry.

Entertainment music firm HMV is expanding its presence in the live music market by buying venue owner

MAMA Group for $46 million. MAMA group runs concert venues including the Hammersmith Apollo in

London. MAMA Group also owns other interests, e.g. an artist management business representing,

artic monkeys etc vaccines business areas.

A force field business model should be constructed with driving and restraining forces identified on

opposing sides in columns to the left and right of a centrally recognised proposal for HMV Group change

to takeover of HAMA Group in music industry.

Each force should have on estimated score noted beside it (1 is the most weak to 5 is the most strong) and these

should be totalled at the bottom of each column. Thus, the questionnaires can analyze how HMV proposed

takeover of MAMA Group will give it a competitive advantage in music market.

HMV music entertainment company needs for a new area of operation to compensate for problems in

traditional areas in music industry.

The Driving forces factors estimated score is needed for change include that it needs enthusiasm of

management, wider market (spreads operational risk), improving profitability aim every year, accessing

to new expertise in MAMA group etc factors.

The restraining forces against factors estimated score for change is who the shareholders need spend

too much cost to approve the takeover include that HMV and MAMA Groups are two different music company. They have differences in corporate cultures need to adapt if HAMA Group wanted takeover

MAMA Group to operate its business successfully, HMA Group needs much time and training to takeover

MAMA Group, it is possible that there is potential staff redundancies change occurrence etc factors.

These are HMV Group external and internal factors to analyse how HMV's proposed takeover of the

MAMA Group will give it a competitive advantage in the music industry.

Chapter nine Explaining international trading management strategies

Q1 Define the term globalisation

Globalization means integration of world economies through free trade, free flow of capital and cheaper

foreign labour markets. The free trade of goods, capital ad labour in worldwide markets. It is

unrestricted by trade barriers, such as tariffs.

On the global stage, competitive advantages are gained by creating, transferring and exploiting competences

across operations and locations internationally.

Economic effects of globalization include global economic growth and distribution.

Globalization results multinational organizations are heavily involved in global changes. Many of these

organizations are pursuing joint ventures with firms from other countries.

Q2 Explain two potential advantages to Kraft of taking over Cadbury

Takeover means one business, usually larger one, buys controlling interest of another business.

Kraft is USA one chocolate and cheese and cake foods sale company, it takes over Cadbury UK chocolate company potential advantages include that instant growth to enter European chocolate market in short term; increasing geographic and chocolate markets expanding to European market spread; acquired European chocolate manufacturing local experts skills and European supply chain contacts to suppliers more easier; acquisition may be at lower than the chocolate market value of the assets if the acquired business is in difficulty.

Q3 Analyze the problems Kraft might experience as it tries to enter the European chocolate market.

Kraft is one USA chocolate, cheese and cake foods sale company, it tries to enter the European chocolate market, it might experience these problems.

It can lack to understand of European local culture to known European clients chocolate taste, it can lack ability to contract and supply a distribution chains to enter European chocolate easily, A lot of European who don't accept to eat America brand chocolate, cheese and cake foods easily, Kraft's American staffs will feel difficult to speak European language to work in European, Kraft's American staffs need to adapt time difference to work in European, different European consumer law regards chocolate, cheese and cake foods product content, spending advertising to attract European consumers.

Q4 Discuss how Ansoff's matrix model might have been useful to Kraft in making the decision to take over Cadbury.

Ansoff's matrix can make the decision to help Kraft to take over Cadbury in chocolate market.

It can help it's business to analyze how to expand market growth and product growth strategies, it

provides a formal basis for logical and systematic analysis to that all options are considered and

Kraft can encourage consideration of alternative strategic options.

Kraft might have these business strategies in making the decision to take over Cadbury.

Market penetration strategy means existing products in existing markets. Although, this strategy has no

applicable to Kraft because Kraft has no it's USA brand chocolates to exist presence in the European chocolate

market.

However, after it takes over Cadbury in European chocolate market successfully, it can increase it Kraft

chocolate numbers to European largely. It is low risk strategy, may be achieved by improving Kraft and

Cadbury chocolate product element mix, promotion can be forced on future European existing clients to

make more purchase.

Market development strategy means existing products enter to new markets. Kraft may see opportunity

to reposition some existing European Cadbury brands chocolate foods to sell to new chocolate market.

For example: Asian countries include Hong Kong, Taiwan, China, Japan etc. It is medium risk strategy,

it can be risky if have little knowledge of the new market, Kraft needs new distribution channels to sell these Asian countries new chocolate markets.

Product development strategy means new products enter new markets. Kraft and Cadbury brand chocolates may to renew to resign their package design and may give discount to pricing to be adapted to these Asian countries new chocolate market. It is medium risk strategy, it may be suitable if Kraft and Cadbury chocolate food products have reached saturation or decline. It is a reason why Kraft acquires Cadbury chocolate business.

Diversification means new products enter in new markets. It is high risk strategy, it can gain market share in existing markets, it is spread risk and it is often a reason why businesses acquire new businesses.

For example, Kraft and Cadbury co-operate to produce new taste of chocolates, cheeses and cake foods to sell to Asia countries, e.g. China, Hong Kong , Japan, Korean etc countries.

Printed by Libri Plureos GmbH in Hamburg, Germany